The Fortune Formula

Unlocking The Millionaire's Code

Lucy Brooks

The Fortune Formula: Unlocking The Millionaire's Code

Lucy Brooks

Other books written by the Author

Youtube Creator's Bible

Science, Christianity, and the AI Revolution: A Christian Perspective

Pips and Profits: Turning Market Moves into Wealth

Table of Contents

The Power of Mindset

Building a Millionaire Mindset

Crafting Visionary Goals

The Power of Mindset

I had spent most of my life navigating the narrow alleyways of financial struggle, haunted by the ghost of scarcity. Bills piled up like insurmountable mountains, and every paycheck seemed to evaporate in the relentless heat of overdue payments. My relationship with money was strained, a dance with scarcity that left me weary and disheartened.

One day, as I walked through the city park feeling the weight of my financial burden, this thought rolled to my heart "I'm wealthy". It all starts within, wealth is an unseen substance, I first of all believe it, work toward it and receive it.

Through discipline and consistency, I established new financial habits. I saved diligently, invested wisely, and made informed decisions about my spending.

The gradual changes in my financial behavior mirrored the internal shifts in my mindset.

Over time, I cultivated patience and embraced delayed gratification. I understood that true abundance was not about instant rewards but rather the culmination of persistent efforts and a steadfast belief in the limitless possibilities of life.

A wealth mindset is a term often used by personal development gurus and financial coaches to describe a mental attitude and belief system that is conducive to attracting and creating wealth. It is based on the idea that our thoughts and beliefs about money and abundance can shape our financial reality.

According to proponents of the wealth mindset, cultivating positive beliefs, attitudes, and habits can lead to financial success and abundance.

However, it is important to approach the concept of a wealth mindset with a critical eye. While mindset can certainly play a role in achieving financial goals, it is not a magic bullet that guarantees instant riches. It is also important to be wary of individuals or courses that promise quick fixes or overnight success.

The idea of a wealth mindset is rooted in the principles of positive psychology and the law of attraction. Positive psychology emphasizes the power of positive thinking and the belief that focusing on strengths and positive emotions can lead to greater well-being and success. According to the law of attraction, positive thinking and beliefs lead to positive outcomes.

To develop a wealth mindset, it is important to start by examining and challenging any negative beliefs or attitudes you may have about money and wealth. This may involve identifying and reframing limiting beliefs, such as "money is evil" or "I will never be rich." Instead, focus on cultivating a mindset of abundance, gratitude, and possibility.

What is the difference between a Millionaire mindset and a scarcity mindset?

"Wealth mindset," or abundant thinking, is the belief that the universe is abundant and our potential is limitless.

"It's about challenging the self-limitation that comes with money or life goals in general to break through the self-limiting barriers to a higher quality of life," says Kristen Euretten, CFP, Founder and CEO, Brooklyn Plans, LLC.

Scarcity mindset is the belief that there is never enough money, no matter how much money we have in our bank account or how much money we pay in our bills. This "not enough" feeling can lead to unhealthy spending habits.

"When it comes to personal finance," says Julie Prince, Founder and CEO, "scarcity mindset refers to the idea that something will only be available for a limited time or at a specific price for a limited time."

For example, during a Black Friday sale or when an online retail store notifies you that they only have two of something in your size left. This is often done as a sales technique to make you believe that this is the last chance to purchase their product at such a low price.

Myths About Millionaire Mindset

Myth 1: You're not enough.

This is patently false. Many life coaches use the anxieties built into the scarcity mindset to sell their courses as a marketing strategy. By making their course material seem like a "now or never" situation, they reinforce the feeling that they are not enough. According to coach Ali Bowman, when you create "certainty" and "urgency," you're often telling people what's wrong with their lives—not what abundant thinking is meant to emphasize. "There's a lot of subtlety in how people use wealth/money to draw in clients when they're actually working on self-love and happiness and confidence," she says. "The general rule I hear in coaching circles is that if it gets you the transformation, you'll say what's needed to get you in the door." Be wary of this marketing tactic. It's feeding your fear.

Myth 2: You don't always get what you pay for

According to Euretig, one of the biggest problems with the influencer/coach culture surrounding this topic is the lack of transparency. "Sometimes influencers don't live the lives they advertise on social media," she says. "I had the chance to observe an influencer who created this kind of content and was drowning in debt without a plan to get out of it."

There's a difference between a "mindset" and a "disconnectedness" with financial reality. Strengthening your financial position is a long-term endeavor, both emotionally and financially. It takes time, effort, and technical expertise. While a mindset is important, so is knowledge, skill, and action.

Myth 3: It promises huge financial gains in a matter of months.

For most people, this is not the case. The ranges of wealth shared by many coaches on Instagram are often inflated and fail to recognize some of the privileges they enjoy.

Jocellyn Harvey, an author and former coach, notes that it can be confusing when a coach promises so much so soon in their courses. "A coach shouldn't promise anything," she says. "The most unrealistic marketing point that some 'guarantee' makes is timing."

"It's not 100 percent impossible for someone to double or triple their income in a matter of six months," Harvey says. "But it doesn't happen for a lot of people." She adds that this can leave clients frustrated when they follow the steps and life remains the same. "These claims don't take into account all the work that someone has done and all the struggles they've gone through to get where they are today."

Myth 4: Wealth is a Solo Journey

Contrary to the popular narrative, building wealth is not solely an individual pursuit. The myth of the lone millionaire who achieved success without any external support perpetuates an unrealistic and isolating expectation. In reality, many successful individuals have benefited from collaboration, mentorship, and a supportive network.

Financial success often involves strategic partnerships, shared knowledge, and leveraging collective resources. Renowned entrepreneur Maria Rodriguez emphasizes the importance of community in wealth-building. Wealth isn't just about making money, it's about building relationships and capitalizing on each other's strengths," he says. The idea that one must navigate the path to prosperity alone neglects the power of collective wisdom and collaborative efforts.

Myth 5: It's All about Sacrifice and Deprivation

Another common misconception in the millionaire mindset narrative is the belief that achieving financial success requires constant sacrifice and a life devoid of enjoyment. The notion that one must endure extreme hardship to accumulate wealth can lead to burnout and dissatisfaction.

Financial expert Mark Thompson challenges this myth, asserting that a balanced and fulfilling life is essential for sustained success. "Wealth is not just about the numbers in your bank account; it's about the quality of life you lead," he explains. Emphasizing the importance of self-care, hobbies, and leisure, Thompson encourages aspiring millionaires to pursue their passions while working towards their financial goals.

12 Principles of Wealth

1. Your income can only grow as you do!
2. To change the fruit, you first need to change the root. To change the visible part, you need to change the invisible part.
3. The world is made up of things like money, wealth, health, disease, your weight, etc.
4. If your reason for wanting money or success is based on fear, anger or the need to prove yourself, then your money will never make you happy.
5. Consciousness is watching what you are thinking and doing so that you can experience true freedom in the

present instead of being controlled by past programming.

6. When you complain, you become a "crap magnet."

7. If you want to be comfortable, you will never be rich. But if you want to be rich, you will be very comfortable.

8. One of the most common reasons why people don't get exactly what they want is because they don't know what they want.

9. If you don't want to create wealth, it's unlikely that you will.

10. If you don't want to create wealth, it's unlikely that you will.

11. Leaders make more money than followers!

12. The key to success isn't getting rid of or shrinking from your issues;

it's growing up so that you're bigger than any issue.

Affirmations and Visualization

An affirmation is a positive statement that you make to yourself every day. They are designed to reprogram your mind with empowering beliefs and thoughts, and help you overcome limiting beliefs and negative self-talk. Affirmations can be used to manifest financial success by focusing on positive outcomes, such as abundance, prosperity, and financial freedom. Here are some tips on how to use affirmations effectively:

1. Choose affirmations that resonate with you. Select affirmations that align with your goals and values, and that feel authentic and empowering.

2. Repeat your affirmations daily. Choose a time of day that works best for you, such as first thing in the morning or before bed.

3. Use present-tense language. Affirmations are most effective when they are stated in the present tense, as if the desired outcome has already occurred.

4. Make it personal. Customize your affirmations to reflect your specific financial goals and desires.

5. Believe it. Trust that your affirmations are true and that they will manifest in your life.

Visualization Techniques

Visualization is another powerful tool for manifesting financial success. Visualization is the process of using your imagination to visualize your desired outcome. By vividly picturing yourself achieving financial success, you can attract that success into your life. Here are some tips for using visualization techniques effectively:

1. Be specific: Visualize specific details of your desired financial outcome, such as the amount of money you want to earn or the specific financial goals you want to achieve.

2. Make it vivid: Use all of your senses to create a vivid mental picture of your desired outcome. See yourself achieving financial success in as much detail as possible. Hear the sound of your success, feel the emotions of joy and fulfillment, and smell the scent of success.

3. Use positive self-talk: As you visualize your success, use positive self-talk to reinforce your belief in yourself. Tell

yourself that you are capable and deserving of financial success.

4. Visualize regularly: Make visualization a regular part of your daily routine. Set aside time each day to visualize your financial success, and make it a habit.

5. Take action. While visualization is powerful, it is not enough on its own. Take action towards your financial goals, and use your visualization practice to motivate and inspire you.

6. Let go of limiting beliefs. Identify any limiting beliefs that may be holding you back from achieving financial success, and let them go. Instead, replace them with belief systems that empower you to reach your financial objectives.

7. Practice gratitude. Gratitude is a powerful tool for manifesting financial success. Practice gratitude by focusing on

the things you are thankful for, and by expressing your gratitude to others.

8. Trust in the universe. Trust that the universe will provide you with the resources and opportunities you need to achieve financial success. Have faith that your financial goals will manifest in the right time.

9. Be patient. Manifesting financial success takes time, and it is important to be patient and persistent. Keep your focus on your goals, and trust that they will manifest in the right time.

10. Celebrate your successes. Celebrate your accomplishments no matter how small or large your accomplishments are, celebrating them will keep you motivated and on track with your financial goals.

Manifesting financial success is a powerful process that can help you achieve your financial goals and live a life of abundance and prosperity.

Building a Millionaire Mindset

Twenty-Nine Ways Rich People Think and Act Differently from Poor People

Millionaire mindset is a set of habits and behaviors that help you achieve financial success. Some of these are: Setting clear goals, Being disciplined with money, Taking calculated risks, Always learning and improving, Being proactive and looking for opportunities, Being surrounded by like-minded individuals, Putting long-term wealth growth ahead of short-term gratification, Being frugal, Investing wisely, Having a positive attitude even when faced with adversity.

These are just a few of the habits that a millionaire has in common. While they may vary from one person to another, they all relate to the principles of Financial Responsibility, Growth mindset, and Strategic Thinking. Here are habits of "millionaire Behaviour" for you to try out:

File 1: Setting Goals

Millionaire thinkers are individuals who have achieved great wealth and success. One of the key characteristics of these individuals is their ability to set clear and ambitious goals to guide their actions. By having a clear vision of what they want to achieve, millionaire thinkers are able to focus their efforts and make strategic decisions that align with their long-term objectives.

Setting clear and ambitious goals is important for several reasons. Firstly, it provides a sense of direction and purpose. When individuals have a clear goal in mind, they have something to work towards and can prioritize their actions accordingly. This helps them stay motivated and committed to their objectives, even when faced with challenges or setbacks.

Secondly, setting ambitious goals pushes individuals to go beyond their comfort zones and strive for excellence. By setting high standards for themselves, millionaire thinkers are constantly challenging themselves to improve and reach new heights. This mindset of continuous improvement is crucial for long-term success and allows individuals to constantly evolve and adapt to changing circumstances.

Clear and ambitious goals provide a framework for decision-making. When faced with various options and opportunities, millionaire thinkers can use their goals as a guiding principle to assess which choices align with their overall vision. This helps them make informed decisions that are in line with their long-term objectives, rather than being swayed by short-term temptations or distractions.

In order to set clear and ambitious goals, millionaire thinkers often employ various strategies. They engage in self-reflection and introspection to identify their passions, values, and strengths. This self-awareness helps them define what they truly want to achieve and what is most important to them.

Additionally, millionaire thinkers break down their goals into smaller, manageable tasks. This allows them to create a roadmap towards their objectives and track their progress along the way. By breaking down big goals into smaller milestones, they are able to maintain focus and stay motivated throughout the journey.

To further support their goal-setting process, millionaire thinkers often seek advice and guidance from mentors or experts in their field. Learning from those who have already achieved success can provide valuable insights and help them refine their goals and strategies.

File 2: Financial Discipline

Financial discipline is an important aspect of personal finance. It involves practicing disciplined spending, saving, and investing in order to build wealth over time. By exercising financial discipline, individuals can effectively manage their money and achieve their long-term financial goals.

Disciplined spending refers to the practice of making thoughtful and intentional purchasing decisions. It involves distinguishing between needs and wants, prioritizing essential expenses, and avoiding impulsive or unnecessary purchases. By being mindful of their spending habits, individuals can control their expenses and allocate their resources towards more meaningful and valuable investments.

Saving plays a crucial role in financial discipline. One way to save money is to set aside a portion of your income for future expenses. It serves as a financial safety net and allows individuals to meet unexpected expenses or achieve specific financial goals. By consistently saving a percentage of their income, individuals can build an emergency fund, plan for retirement, or save for major life events such as purchasing a home or starting a family.

Investing is another key component of financial discipline. By investing, individuals can put their money to work and potentially generate additional income or capital appreciation. There are various investment options available, such as stocks, bonds, mutual funds, real estate, and more. However, it is important to note that investing comes with risks, and individuals should conduct thorough research and seek professional advice before making investment decisions.

In order to practice financial discipline effectively, individuals can implement several strategies. Creating a budget is essential, as it provides a framework for managing income and expenses. A budget helps individuals track their spending, identify areas where they can cut back, and allocate funds towards saving and investing. It is also important to set realistic financial goals and regularly review progress towards achieving them.

Furthermore, establishing an emergency fund is a prudent step towards financial discipline. An emergency fund provides a financial cushion in case of unexpected events, such as job loss, medical emergencies, or major repairs. Having an emergency fund can prevent individuals from relying on high-interest debt or derailing their long-term financial plans.

File 3: Continuous Learning

Continuous learning is a cornerstone of the millionaire mindset, reflecting a deep-seated commitment to acquiring knowledge throughout one's life. This dedication goes beyond formal education and extends into a proactive engagement with the ever-evolving landscape of market trends and opportunities.

Millionaire thinkers understand that the business environment is dynamic, subject to constant shifts influenced by technological advancements, consumer preferences, and global economic changes. To stay ahead in this dynamic landscape, they immerse themselves in a culture of ongoing education. This involves not only formal courses and degrees but also a voracious appetite for self-directed learning.

Remaining informed about market trends is more than just a habit; it's a strategic imperative. Millionaire thinkers recognize that the ability to anticipate shifts in the market provides a competitive edge. They avidly consume industry reports, market analyses, and expert opinions, leveraging this information to make informed decisions that position them for success.

Moreover, their commitment to continuous learning extends to understanding emerging opportunities. Whether it's exploring new technologies, identifying niche markets, or capitalizing on evolving consumer behaviors, these individuals proactively seek out and capitalize on potential avenues for growth.

This mindset of perpetual learning not only ensures they stay relevant but also positions them to innovate and capitalize on emerging trends before they become mainstream.

File 4: Risk - Taking

The millionaire mindset is characterized by a unique relationship with risk—one that transcends the conventional apprehension associated with uncertainty. Instead of shying away from the unknown, individuals with this mindset embrace calculated risks, understanding that the path to success frequently demands stepping outside the familiar confines of one's comfort zone.

At the core of this approach lies a strategic discernment that distinguishes between reckless gambles and well-considered risks. These individuals are adept at evaluating potential outcomes, weighing the probabilities, and meticulously assessing the potential rewards. It's a mindset that thrives on the principle of calculated risk-taking, where decisions are informed by a thorough understanding of the landscape, industry dynamics, and their own capabilities.

Stepping outside the comfort zone becomes a deliberate choice, not a haphazard venture into the unknown. This calculated approach enables them to navigate uncertainties with a degree of confidence, turning what might seem like a leap of faith to others into a strategic move. They recognize that true innovation and growth often lie beyond the familiar, and by embracing calculated risks, they position themselves to capitalize on opportunities that others might perceive as too daunting.

Moreover, the willingness to venture beyond the comfort zone is underpinned by a deep understanding of the correlation between risk and reward. These individuals acknowledge that substantial achievements seldom arise from playing it safe. By daring to tread into uncharted territory, they open themselves up to the potential for significant gains, be it in business ventures, investments, or personal development.

This mindset also cultivates resilience. Embracing calculated risks means acknowledging that setbacks are an inherent part of the journey. Instead of viewing failures as insurmountable obstacles, these individuals see them as valuable learning experiences, integral to the process of growth and achievement.

It's a mindset that not only propels them forward but also fosters a resilience that is vital in the ever-changing landscape of entrepreneurship and innovation.

File 5: Network Building

Network building is a crucial skill in today's interconnected world. It involves establishing and nurturing valuable connections with individuals and organizations, which can provide access to various opportunities and insights. By actively engaging in network building, individuals can expand their knowledge, enhance their professional development, and increase their chances of success in their chosen fields.

One way to build a network is through attending networking events and conferences. These gatherings bring together professionals from different industries and provide a platform for individuals to connect, exchange ideas, and explore potential collaborations. Attending such events allows individuals to meet like-minded individuals, learn from industry experts, and stay updated on the latest trends and developments in their field.

Another effective way to build a network is through online platforms and social media. With the advent of technology, individuals can connect with others from around the world with just a few clicks. Platforms like LinkedIn, Twitter, and Facebook provide opportunities to connect with professionals, join groups and communities, and engage in discussions related to their field of interest. By actively participating in online communities and sharing valuable insights, individuals can establish themselves as thought leaders and expand their network.

Building a network also involves maintaining and nurturing existing connections. Regularly keeping in touch with contacts, whether through emails, phone calls, or meetings, helps to strengthen relationships and keep them up to date with one's professional endeavors. It is important to show genuine interest in others, offer support and assistance whenever possible, and be proactive in seeking opportunities to collaborate or provide value.

Tips for Surrounding Yourself with the Right People and Environments

a. Before you can surround yourself with the right people and environments, you need to have a clear understanding of your financial goals. What do you want to achieve? What kind of life do you envision for yourself and your loved ones?

b. Look for people who are supportive, motivated, and have a positive outlook on life. These individuals can provide encouragement, advice, and resources to help you achieve your financial goals.

c. Joining industry-specific groups or organizations can provide you with access to a network of like-minded individuals who share your interests and goals. These groups can also provide valuable resources, such as mentorship, training, and business opportunities.

d. Attending seminars and workshops can provide you with valuable information and insights on how to achieve your financial goals. These events can also provide opportunities to network with successful individuals in your industry.

e. Surround yourself with reminders of your financial goals, such as pictures or motivational quotes. Create a comfortable and organized workspace that inspires you to take action.

f. Be intentional about the people you spend time with and the environments you surround yourself with. Make a conscious effort to seek out positive influences and avoid negative ones.

g. Taking care of yourself is essential for achieving your financial goals. Make sure to get enough sleep, exercise regularly, and eat a healthy diet. A healthy body and mind can help you stay motivated and focused on your goals.

h. Having a mentor can provide you with valuable guidance and support as you work towards your financial goals. Look for someone who is successful in your industry and who is willing to share their knowledge and experience with you.

i. Be open-minded to new ideas and perspectives. Surrounding yourself with people who have different backgrounds and experiences can provide you with a fresh perspective and help you to think outside the box.

j. Practice gratitude by focusing on the positive aspects of your life and the people around you. This will help you stay focused and on track with your objectives.

k. Stay humble and avoid getting too caught up in your own success. Remember that there is always room for improvement and that you can always learn from others.

l. Give back to your community and to those in need. This can help you to stay grounded and to appreciate the blessings in your life.

m. Stay focused on your goals and avoid distractions. Use tools like a vision board or a to-do list to help you stay on track.

n. Celebrate your successes, no matter how small they may be. This can help you to stay motivated and to feel a sense of accomplishment.

o. Stay positive and avoid negative self-talk. Believe in yourself and your abilities, and remember that setbacks are only temporary.

p. Seek out challenges and step outside of your comfort zone. This can help you to grow and to learn new skills.

q. Practice mindfulness by being present in the moment and focusing on your breath and your surroundings. This can help you to stay calm and focused.

r. Stay connected with your friends and family, and make an effort to build new relationships. This can help you to feel supported and to have a sense of belonging.

s. Take care of yourself by getting enough sleep, eating a healthy diet, and exercising regularly. This can help you to stay energized and focused.

By following these tips, you can create a supportive and motivating environment that will help you to achieve your financial goals and to live a fulfilling life.

File 6: Adaptability

Successful individuals with a millionaire mindset are known for their adaptability. They are quick to recognize and respond to changing circumstances and market conditions. This adaptability allows them to stay ahead of the curve and make informed decisions that can lead to financial success.

In order to adapt effectively, individuals with a millionaire mindset continuously educate themselves and stay up-to-date on industry trends. They understand that the business landscape is constantly evolving, and they strive to stay ahead of the competition by acquiring new knowledge and skills.

Furthermore, individuals with a millionaire mindset are not afraid to take risks and step out of their comfort zone. They understand that in order to achieve success, they must be willing to try new things and embrace change. They are open-minded and flexible, always willing to consider different perspectives and approaches.

Adaptability also involves being able to think critically and problem-solve. Successful individuals with a millionaire mindset are skilled at analyzing situations and finding creative solutions. They are able to quickly assess the situation, identify potential obstacles, and come up with strategies to overcome them.

In addition to these qualities, individuals with a millionaire mindset also possess a strong sense of resilience. They understand that setbacks and failures are inevitable, but they do not let these obstacles deter them. Instead, they see challenges as opportunities to learn and grow.

Adaptability is a key characteristic of successful individuals with a millionaire mindset. Their ability to adapt to changing circumstances and market conditions allows them to stay ahead of the competition and make informed decisions. By continuously educating themselves, taking risks, thinking critically, and embracing change, they are able to achieve financial success.

File 7: Time Management

The emphasis on effective time management is a hallmark of the millionaire mindset, underscoring a keen awareness of the invaluable nature of time and the critical role it plays in achieving both personal and professional goals. This mindset goes beyond the conventional understanding of time management; it embodies a strategic and intentional approach to allocating time resources for maximum productivity and impact.

Individuals with the millionaire mindset understand that time, once spent, cannot be reclaimed. As such, they prioritize their tasks with meticulous precision, recognizing that every minute dedicated to a task is an investment in their journey toward success. This discerning approach involves not only setting clear priorities but also constantly evaluating and adjusting them based on changing circumstances and goals.

The commitment to maximizing productivity is not about simply working harder but working smarter. These individuals are adept at identifying high-impact activities and focusing their energy on tasks that align with their overarching objectives. This strategic allocation of time allows them to make significant strides towards their goals, avoiding the pitfalls of busyness for its own sake. Furthermore, the millionaire mindset recognizes the importance of balancing short-term tasks with long-term objectives. While they are efficient in handling immediate demands, they also dedicate time to strategic planning and visionary thinking. This dual focus ensures that they not only manage their time effectively in the present but also position themselves for sustained success in the future.

In practice, this mindset often involves employing tools and techniques such as prioritization matrices, goal-setting frameworks, and delegation strategies. It's about creating systems that facilitate efficiency and ensure that every moment contributes meaningfully to the overall trajectory of success.

Beyond the professional realm, these individuals extend their time management principles to personal development, relationships, and self-care. They understand that a holistic approach to time management encompasses all facets of life, creating a harmonious balance that nurtures both professional success and personal well-being.

File 8: Positive Mindset

Maintaining a positive and optimistic mindset is crucial for individuals to overcome challenges and stay focused on their goals. A positive mindset enables individuals to approach difficult situations with resilience and determination, allowing them to find creative solutions and persevere through obstacles. It also helps individuals to maintain a sense of motivation and enthusiasm, which can lead to increased productivity and success in various aspects of life.

When individuals have a positive mindset, they are more likely to see setbacks and failures as opportunities for growth and learning. Instead of being discouraged by setbacks, they view them as temporary setbacks and stepping stones towards achieving their goals. This mindset allows individuals to bounce back quickly from failures and setbacks, and continue working towards their objectives with renewed energy and determination.

Maintaining a positive mindset can have a significant impact on mental and emotional well-being. Research has shown that individuals with a positive outlook are less likely to experience symptoms of anxiety and depression. They are better equipped to manage stress and are more resilient in the face of adversity. This is because a positive mindset enables individuals to focus on the positives in their lives, rather than dwelling on negativity or pessimism.

There are a few things you can do to create and sustain a positive attitude. One of the most effective ways is to practice gratitude. Taking time each day to reflect on and appreciate the things that one is grateful for can help shift focus away from negativity and foster a more positive outlook. Engaging in activities that bring joy and fulfillment, such as hobbies or spending time with loved ones, can also contribute to a positive mindset.

It is important to note that maintaining a positive mindset does not mean ignoring or suppressing negative emotions. It is normal and healthy to experience a range of emotions, including sadness, anger, and frustration. However, individuals with a positive mindset are able to acknowledge and process these emotions in a constructive manner, without allowing them to dominate their thoughts and actions.

Maintaining a positive mindset is essential for individuals to overcome challenges and stay focused on their goals. It enables individuals to approach difficult situations with resilience and determination, view setbacks as opportunities for growth, and protect their mental and emotional well-being.

File 9: Multiple Income Streams

Diversifying income sources is a common practice among individuals and businesses, as it helps reduce dependency on a single avenue. Having multiple income streams can provide stability and security, especially during times of economic uncertainty. By diversifying their income sources, individuals can minimize the risk of financial loss and increase their overall earning potential.

One way to diversify income sources is by investing in different asset classes. This can include stocks, bonds, real estate, and commodities. By spreading investments across various asset classes, individuals can benefit from different market conditions and reduce the impact of a downturn in one particular sector. Additionally, investing in different geographic regions can also help mitigate risks associated with a single country or region.

Another strategy for diversifying income sources is by starting a side business or pursuing freelance work. This allows individuals to generate additional income outside of their primary job or career. Side businesses can range from online ventures, such as e-commerce or consulting, to traditional brick-and-mortar establishments. Freelance work, on the other hand, allows individuals to offer their skills and expertise on a project basis, providing a flexible way to earn extra income.

Furthermore, diversifying income sources can also involve passive income streams. Passive income, on the other hand, is income that doesn't require much maintenance. This could be rental income, dividend income, or intellectual property royalties. By generating passive income, individuals can supplement their active income (from employment or self-employment) and create a more stable financial foundation.

Diversifying income sources is a prudent financial strategy that can provide individuals and businesses with increased stability and security. By investing in different asset classes, starting a side business or pursuing freelance work, and generating passive income, individuals can reduce their dependence on a single avenue and increase their overall earning potential. It is important to carefully evaluate and manage each income source to ensure a balanced and diversified portfolio.

File 10: Self-Reflection

The commitment to self-reflection is a distinctive feature of the millionaire mindset, embodying a continuous and intentional process of introspection that extends beyond the realm of achievements and success. Regularly pausing to examine actions and decisions serves as a dynamic tool for learning, growth, and the perpetual refinement of one's approach to both personal and professional endeavors.

Individuals with the millionaire mindset view self-reflection not as an occasional exercise but as an integral part of their daily routine. This deliberate practice involves taking a step back to analyze the motivations behind their actions, dissecting the outcomes, and discerning the lessons embedded in each experience. It's a conscious effort to extract valuable insights that can inform future decisions and shape a more refined and effective approach.

In the context of successes, self-reflection isn't merely a celebration but an exploration of what contributed to the positive outcome. By understanding the elements that led to success, these individuals can replicate and amplify those factors in future endeavors. Conversely, in the face of challenges or setbacks, self-reflection becomes a powerful tool for resilience and adaptation. They scrutinize the circumstances, identify areas for improvement, and view setbacks not as failures but as stepping stones toward greater understanding and achievement.

Moreover, the millionaire mindset's commitment to self-reflection extends beyond the professional realm. It encompasses personal development, relationships, and the alignment of actions with core values. This holistic examination of one's life ensures that success is not pursued at the expense of well-being, integrity, or meaningful connections.

The practice of self-reflection is often facilitated by various tools, such as journaling, mentorship, and seeking feedback from trusted individuals. It's a conscious effort to create a feedback loop that fosters a culture of continuous improvement. By inviting introspection into their daily lives, these individuals cultivate a mindset that thrives on adaptability, resilience, and a genuine desire for personal and professional evolution.

File 11: Leadership Skills

Developing strong leadership skills is essential for effectively managing teams and navigating business challenges.

Leadership skills encompass a wide range of qualities and abilities that enable individuals to guide and inspire others towards achieving common goals. These skills can be developed through various means, including education, training, and experience.

One important aspect of leadership skills is the ability to communicate effectively. Effective communication involves not only conveying information clearly and concisely, but also actively listening to others and understanding their perspectives. By fostering clear and open lines of communication, leaders can build trust and encourage collaboration within their teams.

Another crucial leadership skill is the ability to make sound decisions. Effective leaders are able to analyze complex situations, consider different viewpoints, and arrive at well-informed decisions. They are also willing to take risks when necessary, while also being mindful of the potential consequences. By making timely and informed decisions, leaders can steer their teams towards success.

Leadership skills also include the ability to motivate and inspire others. Effective leaders possess the charisma and vision to inspire their team members to go above and beyond their own expectations. They are able to create a sense of purpose and direction, and instill a shared commitment towards achieving organizational objectives. By motivating and inspiring their team members, leaders can foster a positive and productive work environment.

Leadership skills involve the capacity to adapt and manage change. In today's fast-paced and ever-evolving business landscape, leaders must be adaptable and flexible in order to navigate through uncertainty. They must be open to new ideas and willing to embrace change, while also ensuring that their teams are equipped to handle the challenges that arise.

File 12: Resilience

Resilience is a trait that allows individuals to bounce back from failures and view setbacks as opportunities for growth and learning. When faced with challenges or obstacles, resilient people are able to maintain a positive attitude and persevere through difficult times. They know that failure isn't the end, it's the beginning.

Resilient individuals are able to adapt to change, remain flexible in their thinking, and find creative solutions to problems. This mindset of resilience is essential in navigating the ups and downs of life and achieving personal and professional success.

File 13. Focus on Value

Creating and delivering value to others is a fundamental principle that should be the focus in both business and personal relationships. Value can be defined as the worth, usefulness, or importance that something holds for someone. When we focus on creating and delivering value, we prioritize the needs, desires, and satisfaction of others. This not only helps us build stronger connections and relationships but also enables us to contribute positively to the world around us.

In the context of business, creating value is essential for success. Businesses that prioritize value creation are more likely to attract and retain customers. By understanding the needs and preferences of their target audience, businesses can develop products or services that meet those needs effectively. This can involve innovation, quality improvement, or cost reduction, among other strategies. When customers perceive value in a product or service, they are more likely to choose it over alternatives, leading to increased sales and profitability.

Similarly, in personal relationships, creating value is crucial for building strong connections. When we focus on the needs and desires of others, we show them that we care and value their well-being. This can be done through acts of kindness, support, or simply by being present and attentive. By creating value in our personal relationships, we foster trust, mutual respect, and a sense of belonging. This not only enhances the quality of our relationships but also promotes personal growth and happiness.

To create and deliver value effectively, it is important to understand the specific needs, desires, and preferences of others. This requires active listening, empathy, and a genuine interest in their well-being. By understanding what others value, we can tailor our actions and offerings to meet their expectations. This can involve customizing products or services, providing personalized recommendations, or simply being responsive to feedback. By consistently delivering value, we can build trust, loyalty, and long-term relationships.

File 14: Long-Term Vision

The embodiment of a long-term vision is a fundamental tenet of the millionaire mindset, distinguishing individuals who seek enduring success from those fixated solely on immediate gains. This mindset reflects a strategic approach to life and business, where decisions are guided by a panoramic view of the future rather than a myopic focus on short-term outcomes.

Individuals with the millionaire mindset recognize that success isn't a sprint but a marathon, and as such, they approach their endeavors with a patient and forward-thinking perspective. Instead of succumbing to the allure of quick wins and instant gratification, they meticulously craft and adhere to strategic plans that extend well beyond the immediate horizon.

This commitment to a long-term vision involves setting clear and ambitious goals that transcend the constraints of the present moment. It's about envisioning not only where they want to be in the next quarter or year but also mapping out the trajectory for five, ten, or even twenty years into the future. This farsighted approach provides a roadmap that guides their actions and decisions, ensuring alignment with the overarching vision.

Furthermore, a long-term vision is intricately linked to the cultivation of enduring values and principles. These individuals understand that sustainable success isn't just about financial gains but also about building a legacy, leaving a positive impact on their communities, and contributing to the betterment of society. Their decisions are driven not only by the pursuit of wealth but by a commitment to creating lasting value.

In practice, the millionaire mindset's focus on the long term involves a willingness to make strategic sacrifices in the short term. This might mean forgoing immediate opportunities that don't align with the broader vision or weathering temporary setbacks for the sake of long-term gain. Such decisions are informed by a deep-seated belief in the compounding effect of consistent effort and strategic planning over time.

File 15: Health and Wellness

The millionaire mindset places a profound emphasis on health and wellness, recognizing that the foundation for sustained success and productivity rests on the pillars of physical and mental well-being. This mindset transcends the traditional definition of success, acknowledging that true prosperity encompasses not just financial achievements but a holistic state of being that includes vitality, resilience, and mental clarity.

Individuals with the millionaire mindset understand that their bodies and minds are not just tools for success but essential partners in the journey. The pursuit of physical well-being involves a commitment to regular exercise, a balanced diet, and adequate rest. They view exercise not only as a means to stay fit but as a catalyst for increased energy, heightened focus, and overall well-being. The dietary choices they make are not solely for aesthetic reasons but are consciously selected to fuel their bodies with the nutrients necessary for optimal performance.

Furthermore, mental well-being is regarded as a cornerstone of productivity and success. These individuals prioritize practices that enhance mental clarity, resilience, and emotional intelligence. Techniques such as mindfulness, meditation, and stress management become integral components of their daily routines. By nurturing mental health, they equip themselves to navigate challenges with a composed and strategic mindset, avoiding burnout and maintaining sustained focus on their goals.

The millionaire mindset also acknowledges the interconnectedness of physical and mental well-being. Regular exercise, for example, is not just a physical activity but a powerful stress-reliever and mood enhancer. Adequate sleep is recognized not just for its restorative effects on the body but for its crucial role in cognitive function and decision-making. This holistic approach ensures that both physical and mental aspects are harmonized, creating a synergy that contributes to sustained productivity and success.

The commitment to health and wellness extends beyond personal benefits to impact the overall quality of life. These individuals understand that a healthy lifestyle not only enhances their own performance but also influences the work environment, team dynamics, and the broader community. By prioritizing health, they set an example that encourages those around them to adopt similar habits, fostering a culture of well-being.

File 16: Continuous Improvement

Continuous improvement is a guiding principle for those with the millionaire mindset, representing a relentless commitment to refining and expanding their skills and knowledge throughout their personal and professional journey. This mindset goes beyond the notion of occasional learning; it forms an ingrained habit, an unwavering dedication to staying at the forefront of their field and adapting to the ever-evolving landscape of opportunities and challenges.

Individuals with the millionaire mindset approach each day as an opportunity for growth. They actively seek out ways to enhance their skills, recognizing that in a rapidly changing world, stagnation is not an option.

This perpetual habit involves a proactive pursuit of knowledge through various channels, including books, courses, workshops, and mentorship relationships. They understand that the acquisition of new skills and insights is not just a means to an end but a continuous journey that enriches both their personal and professional lives.

The commitment to continuous improvement is not solely about acquiring new skills but also about refining existing ones. These individuals engage in a process of introspection, regularly evaluating their strengths and weaknesses. By identifying areas that need enhancement, they construct targeted plans for improvement, whether through focused practice, further education, or collaboration with experts in those domains.

Adaptability is a natural byproduct of this mindset. Recognizing that the business landscape is dynamic and subject to rapid changes, millionaire thinkers view adaptability as a competitive advantage. They welcome new technologies, embrace emerging trends, and remain agile in the face of shifting paradigms. This adaptability is not just a survival strategy; it's a proactive stance that positions them to lead and innovate in their respective fields.

In the context of continuous improvement, failure is not a deterrent but a stepping stone to success. These individuals perceive setbacks as invaluable learning experiences, dissecting the reasons behind the failure and leveraging those insights to refine their strategies. The ability to extract lessons from both successes and failures contributes to a resilient mindset that thrives on adversity.

File 17: Innovation

The value of innovation stands as a cornerstone principle, emphasizing the critical importance of embracing change and staying at the forefront of technological advancements. This mindset reflects not only an openness to new ideas but a proactive commitment to leveraging innovation as a driving force in various fields.

For individuals with the millionaire mindset, innovation is not just a buzzword; it's a strategic imperative. They recognize that in an era of rapid technological evolution, complacency can lead to obsolescence. Hence, a proactive approach to innovation becomes integral to their success. This involves not only adopting cutting-edge technologies but actively seeking opportunities to contribute to and shape the trajectory of innovation within their industries.

Staying abreast of technological advancements is a continuous process. These individuals immerse themselves in the ever-expanding landscape of emerging technologies, from artificial intelligence and blockchain to biotechnology and beyond. They understand that a deep understanding of technological trends provides a competitive edge, allowing them to anticipate shifts in the market, identify new opportunities, and navigate the complexities of an evolving business landscape.

Innovation, in the context of the millionaire mindset, extends beyond technology. It encompasses a culture of creative thinking and problem-solving.

These individuals foster an environment that encourages out-of-the-box ideas, values experimentation, and views failures as valuable learning experiences. This mindset permeates not only their approach to business but also their personal development, relationships, and community engagement.

Innovation is not seen as a solitary pursuit. Collaborative efforts, partnerships, and networking are integral components of the innovation process. Millionaire thinkers understand that diverse perspectives and collaborative ventures enhance the potential for groundbreaking ideas. They actively engage with thought leaders, participate in industry forums, and seek opportunities for interdisciplinary collaboration to drive innovation forward.

File 18: Mindful Spending

The practice of mindful spending is a deliberate and integral aspect of the millionaire mindset, embodying a conscientious awareness of financial decisions and a commitment to aligning expenditures with overarching financial goals. Far beyond mere frugality, mindful spending is a strategic approach that involves thoughtful consideration of how each expenditure contributes to long-term financial well-being.

Individuals with the millionaire mindset recognize that money is a finite resource and that every spending choice has implications for their financial trajectory. Mindful spending starts with a clear understanding of financial goals, whether it be saving for investments, debt reduction, or building a financial safety net. This clarity serves as a guiding principle, shaping spending decisions in a way that advances, rather than hinders, these objectives.

Moreover, mindful spending involves a keen awareness of needs versus wants. These individuals differentiate between essential expenses that contribute to their well-being and goals and discretionary spending that may provide temporary satisfaction but doesn't align with their overarching financial plan. This discernment allows them to allocate resources in a manner that maximizes the impact on their financial health.

Budgeting becomes a proactive tool in the arsenal of mindful spenders. Rather than viewing budgeting as a restrictive practice, they see it as a roadmap that guides their financial journey. Budgets are not static but dynamic, subject to regular reviews and adjustments based on changing circumstances, financial goals, and priorities. This flexibility ensures that their spending remains in harmony with their evolving financial aspirations.

The millionaire mindset's approach to mindful spending extends beyond personal finances to business and investment decisions. Whether it's allocating funds for a new venture, assessing the return on investment, or evaluating business expenses, the same principles of conscious decision-making apply. Every financial choice is examined through the lens of its potential impact on long-term financial success.

Mindful spending is also intertwined with a long-term perspective. Instead of succumbing to impulsive purchases for short-lived gratification, individuals with the millionaire mindset evaluate the lasting value of their expenditures. This forward-looking approach ensures that resources are directed toward endeavors that contribute not just to immediate satisfaction but to sustained financial well-being.

Ultimately, mindful spending is not about deprivation but about empowerment. It's a conscious choice to wield financial resources as a tool for achieving broader objectives. By integrating mindfulness into their spending habits, individuals with the millionaire mindset position themselves for financial success, fostering a culture of responsibility and intentionality that resonates across various aspects of their lives.

File 19: Gratitude

Gratitude is not just a fleeting emotion for those with the millionaire mindset; it is a foundational principle that permeates their outlook on life and success. This mindset recognizes the transformative power of expressing gratitude, understanding that acknowledging achievements and opportunities creates a positive mental environment that, in turn, attracts more success and abundance.

At its core, gratitude for individuals with the millionaire mindset is a conscious and regular practice. It involves taking the time to reflect on accomplishments, big or small, and expressing appreciation for the opportunities that have paved the way for growth and achievement. This intentional reflection isn't limited to personal successes but extends to recognizing the contributions of others, fostering a culture of gratitude within professional and personal spheres.

The expression of gratitude serves as a powerful mindset shift. Instead of fixating solely on future goals or potential challenges, individuals with the millionaire mindset pause to acknowledge the progress they've made. This positive reflection not only instills a sense of accomplishment but also cultivates a mindset of abundance—an understanding that there is already much to be thankful for.

Importantly, the millionaire mindset views gratitude not as a passive reaction but as an active force that shapes future outcomes. By expressing gratitude, individuals invite a positive energy into their lives. This positivity becomes a magnet for more opportunities, success, and meaningful connections. The mindset of abundance that gratitude fosters attracts resources, collaborators, and circumstances that align with their aspirations.

Furthermore, the practice of gratitude contributes to resilience in the face of challenges. Rather than dwelling on setbacks, individuals with the millionaire mindset appreciate the lessons embedded in difficulties and express gratitude for the opportunity to learn and grow. This adaptive mindset transforms adversity into a stepping stone for future success.

In professional and leadership roles, the millionaire mindset extends gratitude beyond individual achievements to the collective efforts of teams. Recognizing and appreciating the contributions of others not only motivates team members but also strengthens the collaborative spirit, creating a positive and high-performing work environment.

File 20: Be patient

Cultivating patience is a vital virtue on the path to personal and professional development. In a world that often glorifies instant success and rapid achievements, understanding the importance of patience becomes a grounding principle for individuals striving towards their goals.

The journey towards success is often likened to a marathon rather than a sprint. It's natural to feel the weight of impatience when it seems like efforts aren't immediately yielding results. The temptation to rush progress can be overwhelming, especially in a society that often values speed over substance. However, the mindset of patience is a resilient shield against the frustration that may accompany a seemingly slow journey.

The sensation of hustling without immediate rewards can be disheartening, but it's crucial not to let this deter focus and determination. Patience is not passive waiting; it's an active endurance, a persistent commitment to the pursuit of long-term goals despite the absence of instant gratification. It's the understanding that enduring challenges and setbacks is an intrinsic part of the journey, not a signal to abandon the path.

The realization that life-changing transformations don't occur overnight is a powerful anchor. The process of reshaping one's life is intricate and requires sustained effort over time. Personal development, career growth, and achieving significant milestones demand dedication, consistency, and, above all, patience. The acknowledgment that meaningful change is a gradual evolution helps to maintain perspective during moments of frustration.

Setting personal development goals is a commendable endeavor, but it's equally important to recognize that timelines may need to be flexible. Life is unpredictable, and circumstances may evolve in unforeseen ways. It's okay if goals aren't met precisely when initially anticipated. Patience involves understanding that progress is nonlinear and that setbacks are not permanent roadblocks but opportunities for recalibration and learning.

Good things, by their nature, take time to mature. The seed of effort needs the nurturing of time, consistency, and resilience before it blossoms into fruition. The path to success is often characterized by twists and turns, requiring individuals to weather storms and stay committed to their objectives. Patience, in this context, becomes a companion on the journey, offering solace during moments of uncertainty and reminding individuals that their efforts are not in vain.

In essence, the mantra "good things take time" is a profound reminder that the journey towards success is a process, not an event. Patience is not just a virtue but a guiding principle that encourages individuals to persevere, stay focused on their goals, and maintain faith in the transformative power of sustained effort over time. Just because progress may not align with immediate desires doesn't mean it won't happen—patience ensures that the journey unfolds as it should, with each step contributing to a more profound and enduring success.

File 21: Accept mistakes as they come

Embracing mistakes as an integral part of personal and professional growth is a testament to a resilient and growth-oriented mindset. The understanding that mistakes are not mere obstacles but invaluable opportunities for learning and development fundamentally reshapes one's approach to challenges and setbacks.

To grow and learn, one must confront the inevitability of making mistakes. It's a recognition that the journey towards improvement is not a flawless ascent but a dynamic process marked by missteps and course corrections. Viewing mistakes as an inherent part of this journey shifts the narrative from one of fear and avoidance to one of curiosity and adaptation.

Rather than regarding mistakes as things to be avoided at all costs, individuals with this mindset understand that each misstep is an opportunity to learn, adapt, and refine their approach. Mistakes become a teacher, offering insights that success alone may not provide. The acknowledgment that failures are an integral aspect of the learning process allows for a more constructive and positive perspective.

It's crucial to discern between sloppy mistakes that result from carelessness and those that stem from well-intentioned plans that didn't unfold as anticipated. While the former should indeed be avoided through diligence and attention to detail, the latter represents a different category of mistakes—ones that provide valuable information and insight. Plans that don't work out become stepping stones to a more informed and strategic approach, offering the chance to refine tactics and enhance decision-making in the future.

Failures, rather than being viewed as setbacks, are seen as opportunities to gain a deeper understanding of oneself and one's team. The reflective process that follows a mistake becomes a crucial step in the learning journey. By examining the factors that contributed to the misstep, individuals glean valuable insights into their decision-making processes, strengths, and areas that may require improvement.

Moreover, mistakes offer a unique opportunity to develop new skills. Confronting challenges head-on and learning from failures builds resilience, adaptability, and problem-solving capabilities. It's through overcoming obstacles that individuals discover untapped potential and acquire the skills necessary for navigating future uncertainties.

Instead of dwelling on mistakes, individuals with this mindset choose to reflect on them purposefully. This reflective process involves understanding the root causes of the mistake, evaluating the decision-making process, and identifying lessons that can be applied moving forward. Accepting mistakes as part of the growth journey positions individuals to embrace a continuous improvement mindset and fortifies them against the fear of failure.

File 22: Don't forget about sleep

Prioritizing adequate and quality sleep is a fundamental aspect of maintaining overall well-being and optimizing productivity. In the hustle and bustle of our daily lives, it's easy to underestimate the significance of a good night's sleep, often viewing it as a luxury rather than a necessity. However, the millionaire mindset recognizes that to deliver our best work and achieve sustained success, taking care of our physical and mental health through sufficient sleep is non-negotiable.

In the relentless pursuit of our goals, it's not uncommon to encounter days filled with a seemingly endless to-do list. The temptation to sacrifice sleep to accommodate additional work hours may arise, driven by the belief that pushing ourselves harder will lead to increased productivity. However, the millionaire mindset challenges this notion, acknowledging that such an approach is neither sustainable nor conducive to optimal performance.

The understanding that catching up on sleep is a rejuvenating practice for both mind and body is a cornerstone of this mindset. It rejects the notion of burning the midnight oil as a badge of honor and instead advocates for a balanced approach that values rest as an essential component of success. The idea of catching up on sleep is not just about physical recuperation; it's a strategic investment in cognitive function, emotional well-being, and sustained energy levels.

Recognizing that pushing too hard and sacrificing sleep is counterproductive, the millionaire mindset encourages individuals to make the mindful choice of prioritizing rest. Even when faced with a demanding schedule and a sense of urgency to accomplish tasks, it promotes the understanding that an extra hour of work is likely to lead to diminishing returns. Rather than pushing through exhaustion, choosing sleep becomes a conscious decision to enhance productivity and mental clarity.

Moreover, the relationship between sleep and motivation is deeply intertwined. A well-rested body and mind are more likely to be motivated, focused, and ready to tackle the challenges of the day. In contrast, sleep deprivation can lead to a decline in cognitive function, reduced creativity, and increased irritability—factors that hinder rather than support the pursuit of ambitious goals.

In essence, the millionaire mindset recognizes that success is not just about working harder but working smarter. Prioritizing sleep is not a compromise but a strategic choice that enhances overall performance and well-being. By valuing the importance of rest, individuals with this mindset position themselves to navigate challenges with clarity, resilience, and sustained motivation—a combination essential for achieving enduring success in the dynamic landscape of personal and professional endeavors.

File 23: Keep growth in mind

Embarking on the journey toward both professional and personal growth is akin to stepping onto a transformative path where continuous learning and evolution become the guiding principles. Within the expansive landscape of goals, maintaining a growth mindset becomes not just a mindset but a compass, crucial for navigating the inevitable challenges and celebrating the milestones along the way.

The recognition that growth is an inherent part of the journey is foundational to the millionaire mindset. It's an acknowledgment that success is not just about achieving a set of predefined objectives but about becoming a better, more capable individual throughout the process. Keeping a growth mindset is a conscious decision to approach challenges with curiosity, resilience, and an unwavering belief in one's capacity for improvement.

For those with long-term goals, periodic reflection becomes a vital practice. Taking the time to review progress is not merely a check-in on achievements but a celebration of the journey. It offers a moment to appreciate how far you've come, recognizing the accumulation of experiences, skills, and insights gained along the way. This reflection not only instills a sense of accomplishment but also serves as a powerful motivator for the road ahead.

In moments of discouragement, which are inherent in any ambitious pursuit, breaking down long-term goals into manageable tasks becomes a practical strategy. Dividing the journey into smaller, more achievable milestones makes progress feel tangible and allows for a sense of accomplishment with each completed task. This incremental approach not only boosts motivation but also provides clarity on the next steps in the larger journey.

Growth, by its nature, is a gradual and iterative process that unfolds over time. It requires sustained effort, resilience in the face of setbacks, and a commitment to continuous learning. The millionaire mindset recognizes that success is not an overnight phenomenon but the result of persistent hard work and dedication. Acknowledging the journey of growth becomes a source of pride, a reminder of the effort invested, and the resilience demonstrated in the pursuit of one's goals.

Thinking about personal and professional growth becomes a source of inspiration and encouragement. It's a reflection on the challenges overcome, the lessons learned, and the skills honed. This introspective perspective provides a profound sense of pride and accomplishment, instilling the confidence to face future challenges with the same determination that has propelled the journey thus far.

File 24: Stop making excuses for yourself

Eliminating the habit of making excuses is a powerful commitment to personal and professional growth, underscoring the importance of taking responsibility for one's actions and choices. The millionaire mindset thrives on accountability, recognizing that excuses act as hindrances to progress and impede the journey toward achieving ambitious goals.

Excuses have the insidious power to become barriers to success, hindering individuals from pushing forward and realizing their full potential. The first step in breaking free from the cycle of excuses is to confront problems head-on. Instead of deflecting responsibility or laying blame on external factors, adopting time-tested problem-solving techniques becomes the proactive strategy.

When faced with challenges or setbacks, it's essential to resist the inclination to make excuses and, instead, focus on addressing the root of the problem. This involves a shift in mindset from a victim mentality to one of empowerment. Rather than dwelling on the barriers, individuals with the millionaire mindset actively seek solutions and take ownership of their circumstances.

Working with a trusted coach or mentor becomes a valuable resource in this journey. Seeking guidance from someone with experience and a broader perspective can provide insights into what may be holding you back or causing challenges. A mentor or coach can offer constructive feedback, challenge limiting beliefs, and help you formulate effective strategies for overcoming obstacles.

Furthermore, the emphasis on making behavior changes is a key component of eliminating excuses. This requires a commitment to self-awareness and a willingness to adjust actions and approaches as needed. Whether it involves asking for help, altering your methodology, or even taking a temporary break to reassess, the focus is on actively engaging in behaviors that contribute to positive change.

It's crucial to understand that excuses, if allowed to fester, can become a pervasive force that impedes progress. The millionaire mindset recognizes that succumbing to excuses is the worst disservice one can do to oneself. Rather than letting excuses consume your mindset, take charge of your narrative. Recognize that setbacks are opportunities for growth, and challenges are invitations to innovate and adapt.

The decision to stop making excuses is a commitment to personal accountability and a refusal to be held back by self-imposed limitations. It's an acknowledgment that challenges are inherent in any ambitious pursuit, but the true measure of success lies in how one responds to and overcomes these challenges.

File 25: Adopt a "now" mentality

Acknowledging the virtue of patience, the millionaire mindset introduces a dynamic dimension to wealth-building by actively embracing new opportunities. The recognition that seizing these chances might entail temporary financial losses doesn't deter individuals driven by this mindset. Instead, they view such setbacks as investments in a broader spectrum of experiences and connections that ultimately contribute to personal and professional development.

Wealthy individuals stand out not just for their financial acumen but for their proactive approach to identifying and capitalizing on opportunities. Rather than passively waiting for success to unfold, they actively seek out new ventures, recognizing that each opportunity presents a unique pathway for growth and enrichment. This mindset shatters the notion that caution is always the safest route and instead encourages individuals to be vigilant for openings that align with their aspirations.

It's understood within the millionaire mindset that not every opportunity will result in immediate financial gain. Some endeavors may even lead to temporary financial setbacks. However, this mindset is not solely fixated on short-term monetary returns. It values the diverse array of opportunities that may not be immediately revenue-based, such as participating as a speaker at events or volunteering to assist a startup. These experiences, although not immediately lucrative, are viewed as investments in building a multifaceted skill set and expanding one's network.

The connection between experience and opportunity is integral to this mindset. The belief is that the more actively engaged one is in pursuing diverse experiences, the greater the chances of personal and professional development. Engaging with new opportunities contributes not only to skill acquisition but also to the cultivation of a mindset that thrives in dynamic and evolving landscapes. It's an acknowledgment that each experience, regardless of its outcome, holds potential lessons and insights that contribute to an individual's overall growth.

Networking is a natural byproduct of actively pursuing opportunities. The more an individual engages in different ventures, the broader their network becomes. This interconnectedness is seen as a valuable asset, opening doors to collaborations, mentorship, and a wealth of shared knowledge. The millionaire mindset recognizes that success is often a collective effort, and a well-established network can serve as a catalyst for future opportunities.

File 26: Believe in yourself

To build wealth, it's crucial to believe that you have control over your life, especially when it comes to finances. If you think you lack control, it implies a mindset that hinders financial success. This attitude is often seen in people who spend a significant amount on the lottery, hoping luck will bring them wealth. While everyone dreams of winning, those truly on the path to wealth don't rely on the lottery as their main strategy. They understand that personal effort and choices play a more significant role.

Believing in your ability to shape your success is essential. Whether you're aware of it or not, you are the driving force behind your outcomes. Unfortunately, some people, particularly those with financial struggles, tend to adopt a victim mentality. Instead of taking responsibility, they see themselves as helpless. This victim mindset reinforces a cycle of difficulties.

Embracing the millionaire mindset is not a quick fix or a fleeting trend but a steadfast commitment to a set of principles that transcend momentary successes. It's a journey that requires time, dedication, and an unwavering belief in oneself. This fundamental tenet of the millionaire mindset is anchored in the conviction that success is not an overnight achievement but a gradual realization of aspirations.

Believing in oneself is a cornerstone of the millionaire mindset, acknowledging that the path to financial prosperity and personal fulfillment may unfold over a timeline that exceeds initial expectations. Patience becomes a companion on this journey, urging individuals to persevere even when results may not materialize as quickly as desired. The belief in one's ability to reach lofty goals is not contingent on immediate outcomes but on the steadfast dedication to the principles that define the millionaire mindset.

In the pursuit of financial success, it's crucial to internalize the understanding that the journey may take more time than initially anticipated. The millionaire mindset encourages individuals to transcend the pressure of instant gratification and focus on the long-term vision. This requires a commitment to continuous improvement, learning, and adaptability—a recognition that personal and financial growth is a dynamic process that evolves over time.

The self-belief embedded in the millionaire mindset serves as a constant source of motivation during moments of doubt or impatience. It's a reminder that setbacks and delays are inherent in any ambitious pursuit, and they don't diminish the potential for future success. Instead of fixating on immediate outcomes, individuals are encouraged to channel their energy into consistently giving their best effort.

Acknowledging that progress may take time, the millionaire mindset instills a sense of confidence in the incremental steps taken toward the ultimate goal. It's about recognizing and celebrating each small victory along the way, whether it's a financial milestone, a personal achievement, or a moment of self-discovery. Believing in oneself means embracing the journey with resilience and maintaining a positive outlook, even when faced with challenges.

The understanding that you're doing your best is a pivotal aspect of the millionaire mindset. It's a compassionate acknowledgment that the pursuit of success is a demanding endeavor, and individuals should commend themselves for the dedication and effort invested. Recognizing one's best efforts as a commendable achievement fosters a sense of self-worth and encourages individuals to persist with determination and confidence.

File 27: Never trust luck

Adhering to the principle of never trusting luck is a strategic foundation within the millionaire mindset—a mindset that recognizes the importance of proactive planning, foresight, and prudent decision-making. Confidence and a stellar career trajectory are undoubtedly valuable assets, but the millionaire mindset goes beyond relying on these alone, advocating for a meticulous approach to contingencies and financial preparedness.

The understanding that confidence and success do not exempt individuals from unforeseen challenges is integral to the millionaire mindset. While it's essential to celebrate achievements and cultivate a positive trajectory, planning for contingencies is a hallmark of strategic thinking. Envisioning worst-case scenarios becomes a proactive exercise, allowing individuals to identify potential vulnerabilities and develop comprehensive plans to mitigate or navigate through challenges.

The acknowledgment that economic uncertainties, such as recessions or layoffs, are inherent in the dynamic landscape of career and finance is a key aspect of this mindset. Instead of succumbing to the whims of fortune, individuals are encouraged to take a proactive stance. This involves not only preparing for potential setbacks but also actively working to avoid them. By staying attuned to industry trends, economic indicators, and potential risks, individuals position themselves to make informed decisions and adapt swiftly to changing circumstances.

Financial preparedness is a central tenet of the millionaire mindset, emphasizing the importance of saving beyond what the budget strictly requires. This intentional approach to saving serves as a safety net, ensuring that individuals have the financial resources to weather unexpected challenges or seize opportunities. It's a recognition that financial stability is not just about meeting immediate needs but about building a robust foundation that can withstand the uncertainties of the future.

Creating a plan for dealing with worst-case scenarios involves a comprehensive assessment of potential risks and the formulation of strategies to address them. Whether it's a sudden job loss, a market downturn, or other unforeseen challenges, having a well-thought-out contingency plan provides individuals with a roadmap for navigating through turbulent times. This proactive mindset not only instills a sense of preparedness but also positions individuals to respond with resilience and adaptability when faced with adversity.

The principle of never trusting luck within the millionaire mindset is a call to action—a call to actively shape one's destiny rather than leaving it to chance. It's a commitment to strategic planning, foresight, and financial prudence. By envisioning worst-case scenarios, creating comprehensive contingency plans, and saving beyond immediate needs, individuals with the millionaire mindset not only mitigate risks but also cultivate a mindset of resilience and proactivity, ensuring that they are well-prepared for the unpredictable journey of life and career.

File 28: Think big!

A trainer at our seminar shared a powerful story of going from a net worth of $35,000 to over $48 million in just 2 years. When asked about the secret to this success, he attributed it to thinking big. This aligns with the Law of Income, which states that your earnings are directly proportional to the value you provide in the marketplace.

The term "value" is crucial, and four factors determine it: supply, demand, quality, and quantity. Quantity, or how much value you deliver to the marketplace, is often the most challenging for people.

Consider network marketing—there's a notable income difference between someone with ten people in their down-line and someone with ten thousand. The key is playing in the big leagues and affecting more lives.

My experience with a chain of fitness stores illustrates this point. My goal was to have one hundred successful stores and impact twelve of thousands of people. A competitor aimed for just one successful store and earned a decent living. The choice is yours: play big or play small. Fear of failure or success often holds people back, along with feelings of unworthiness.

Your life is not just about you; it's also about contributing to others and living true to your mission. Adding value to people's lives is essential for true richness. Buckminster Fuller once said, "Our mission is to make a difference in the lives of this generation and the generations to come." Your natural talents are meant to be shared, contributing to your mission.

As an entrepreneur, defined as a problem solver, think about whether you want to solve problems for more or fewer people. The more people you help, the richer you become in various aspects—mentally, emotionally, spiritually, and financially. Every person has a mission, and if you're breathing, you're not done. Many people play small due to fear, not fulfilling their duty. The question is: If it's not you, then who else? Your unique purpose may involve real estate investment, helping families find affordable housing. The key is to play big by assisting more families and making a broader impact.

Establishing a clear and well-defined goal serves as the guiding star within the millionaire mindset—a mindset that recognizes the power of purpose in driving motivation and sustaining momentum. Linking every daily task to the overarching objective not only provides direction but also imbues each action with significance, fostering a sense of purpose that fuels determination and hard work.

The process begins with crafting a goal that is specific, measurable, achievable, relevant, and time-bound (SMART). This goal becomes the focal point around which daily tasks orbit. The millionaire mindset emphasizes the importance of clarity in defining this objective, ensuring that it aligns with personal and professional aspirations. It serves as a beacon, illuminating the path to success and providing a framework for strategic decision-making.

Attributing every daily task to the progress of this overarching goal creates a sense of purpose in each action. Whether it's a small task or a significant project, individuals with the millionaire mindset recognize that each contributes to the larger narrative of success. This intentional alignment transforms routine activities into meaningful steps toward the realization of the envisioned goal.

However, the journey towards any goal is not always smooth. Moments of feeling stuck or losing sight of the purpose are natural occurrences. This is where the power of self-reminders comes into play within the millionaire mindset. Regularly revisiting the clear vision of the goal serves as a potent tool for reigniting enthusiasm and energy. It acts as a reminder of the "why" behind the hard work and dedication, reconnecting individuals with the profound purpose that propels them forward.

In moments of challenge or doubt, the vision of the overarching goal becomes a source of motivation. It is a mental anchor that renews commitment and provides clarity amid ambiguity. The millionaire mindset encourages individuals to cultivate the habit of visualizing success, allowing the envisioned goal to serve as a constant source of inspiration, especially during challenging times.

The process of reminding oneself of the overarching vision involves intentional reflection and visualization. It's about immersing oneself in the future state of success, experiencing the emotions associated with achieving the goal, and using this mental imagery to fuel determination and resilience. This practice becomes a powerful strategy for maintaining a positive mindset and overcoming obstacles on the path to success.

Creating a clear goal and aligning every daily task with this objective is not just a strategic approach; it's a transformative mindset. It's about understanding the profound "why" behind the hard work and using this purpose to stay motivated and resilient. By consistently reminding oneself of the vision, individuals with the millionaire mindset not only navigate challenges with purpose but also infuse every action with a sense of meaning that propels them toward enduring success.

File 29: Keep love in mind

Amid the fervent pursuit of goals and the demands of a relentless work ethic, it's all too common to lose sight of the fundamental aspects of life that truly matter, such as mental health and relationships. Within the millionaire mindset, a poignant reminder emerges: keep love in mind. This isn't just a sentimental notion; it's a recognition that personal well-being is intricately tied to social health—a principle substantiated by research linking strong social connections to longevity, stress reduction, and improved heart health.

In the midst of the hustle, it's crucial to prioritize mental health and relationships. The millionaire mindset advocates for a holistic approach to success that encompasses not just professional achievements but also the well-being of the individual. Acknowledging that personal fulfillment extends beyond career accomplishments, individuals are encouraged to foster and cherish meaningful connections with friends, family, and coworkers.

Research underscores the profound impact of strong social connections on various aspects of health. From enhancing overall life expectancy to mitigating the effects of stress and contributing to heart health, the benefits of nurturing relationships are far-reaching. The millionaire mindset understands that sustained success is not just about individual achievements; it's about creating a life of fulfillment and balance, where personal well-being is a priority.

Keeping friends, family, and coworkers in mind becomes a deliberate and conscious practice within the millionaire mindset. This involves actively engaging with loved ones, understanding their aspirations, and providing support in their endeavors. In return, this interconnected focus on relationships creates a reciprocal cycle of inspiration and encouragement. As individuals work toward their goals, the support and inspiration they receive from their social network become powerful motivators, propelling them forward with renewed vigor.

The emphasis on love within the millionaire mindset is not solely about romantic love; it encompasses the broader spectrum of meaningful connections. These connections serve as anchors during challenging times, providing emotional support and perspective. The mindset recognizes that success is richer when shared, and the journey is more meaningful when experienced in the company of those who matter.

Furthermore, the focus on love extends to the workplace, acknowledging the significance of positive relationships with colleagues. A collaborative and supportive work environment contributes not only to individual success but also to the overall success of a team or organization. The millionaire mindset fosters a culture where individuals uplift each other, share insights, and collectively strive for excellence.

How to Identify Self-Imposed Limitations

a. Pay attention to your inner dialogue and identify any negative or limiting beliefs that may be holding you back.

b. Be aware of any patterns of thought that may be limiting your financial growth, such as a fixed mindset or a belief that success is not possible.

c. Examine past experiences that may have reinforced self-imposed limitations and how they may be impacting your current financial situation.

Understanding the Root Causes of Self-Imposed Limitations

a. Reflect on where the self-imposed limitation originated from, such as a past experience or a belief inherited from family or society.

b. Evaluate the beliefs and values that underlie the self-imposed limitation and determine if they are still relevant and serving your financial growth.

c. Understand how emotions such as fear, anxiety, or shame may be contributing to the self-imposed limitation.

Reframing Self-Imposed Limitations

a. Challenge limiting beliefs: Question and challenge any negative or limiting beliefs that may be holding you back.

b. Reframe negative thoughts: Replace negative thoughts with positive, empowering ones that support your financial growth.

c. Practice positive affirmations: Repeat positive affirmations regularly to reinforce new, empowering beliefs and thought patterns.

d. Seek support: Surround yourself with supportive people who will encourage and motivate you to overcome self-imposed limitations.

Turning Self-Imposed Limitations into Catalysts for Abundance

a. Celebrate your individuality and the unique strengths and talents that you bring to the table.

b. Focus on your strengths and use them to your advantage in pursuing financial growth and abundance.

c. Embrace the idea that your abilities and intelligence can be developed through hard work, dedication, and persistence.

d. Cultivate a sense of gratitude for what you already have, and recognize that abundance is not just about money, but also about the people, experiences, and things that bring joy and fulfillment to your life.

e. Step out of your comfort zone and take calculated risks to pursue financial growth and abundance.

f. Recognize that failure is a natural part of growth and learning, and that every setback is an opportunity to learn and improve.

g. Focus on the positive aspects of your life and the world around you, and cultivate a mindset that is open, optimistic, and resilient.

h. Take care of your physical, emotional, and spiritual well-being, and recognize that self-care is not selfish, but essential to living a fulfilling and abundant life.

i. Contribute to the greater good and give back to your community, recognizing that abundance is not just about personal success, but also about making a positive impact on the world around you.

Practical Ways to Use Wealth Mindset

When used correctly, wealth mindset is a powerful way to heal our relationship with money and help us move away from the mindset of scarcity. For many, money is a source of stress and fear that can prevent us from ever feeling truly liberated financially.

"The key to achieving your long-term goals is to change your mindset around money," Prince explains. "It's not the only change you'll need to make, but it's one of the right ones."

For example, Harvey recommends putting together a vision board with pictures of what you really want. Hold onto the photos for a few days or even a few weeks. Take a deep breath and listen to how you feel. "Sometimes you don't want the item you're looking for," she says. "You may find that you're actually happy with what you already have. In that case, saving is a result of gratitude, not fear."

In other cases, you may find that, after a period of time, you really do want the product. Instead of making a hasty purchase, Harvey explains, you have engaged in something more meaningful: intentional spending. "When we spend because we want to spend," says Harvey, "it becomes a slippery slope that doesn't serve our emotional and financial well-being. Intentional spending and gratitude are great examples of practicing a wealthy mindset."

A Lifetime Process

Achieving financial wellness is not a one-off deal. It's something you have to work on and build into your life until it becomes a habit. Once you have a solid financial footing, you can keep track of your progress, Harvey says. "Don't think that after taking one course in money mindset, you will never have any problems again," he says. "This kind of thinking drives people to take courses over and over again because they think they're making mistakes."

Every Path Is Unique

There are no "one-size-fits-all" solutions to financial wellness, Prince says. "Everyone's financial situation is unique, so there's no such thing as a 'quick fix' that works for everyone," he says. "However, if you're looking to improve your financial health, there are a few things you can start with, such as not spending more than your income, starting an emergency savings plan, paying off debt and saving for retirement."

Crafting Visionary Goals

To have a clear vision of the financial future, a person should desire a combination of financial stability, growth, and flexibility. Financial stability refers to having a solid foundation of savings and investments that can provide a safety net during unexpected expenses or economic downturns. It involves having a budget in place, managing debts responsibly, and ensuring a steady income stream.

Financial growth is another important aspect of a clear financial vision. This involves setting goals for increasing wealth, such as saving for retirement, buying a home, or starting a business. It requires making strategic investment decisions, diversifying one's portfolio, and taking advantage of opportunities for growth.

Flexibility is also crucial in envisioning the financial future. This means being adaptable and open to change, as financial circumstances can evolve over time. It involves being prepared for unexpected expenses, having an emergency fund, and being willing to adjust financial plans as needed.

In order to establish a vision that resonates with our deepest aspirations, it is essential to engage in a process of introspection and reflection. This involves delving into our core values, passions, and beliefs to uncover what truly matters to us. By understanding our personal or organizational identity and purpose, we can craft a vision that encapsulates our deepest aspirations.

Once a vision is defined, it is crucial to communicate and share it effectively. This ensures that all stakeholders are aware of the direction in which we are heading and can actively contribute towards its realization. Clear and concise communication of the vision fosters a sense of unity and purpose, motivating individuals to work towards the common goal.

Setting goals that align with the vision is the next step in the process. These objectives should be strategic, measurable, attainable, pertinent, and time-aligned (SMART). By breaking down the vision into smaller, actionable goals, we can develop a roadmap that guides our progress. Each goal should contribute to the overall vision and serve as a stepping stone towards its fulfillment.

In order to ensure the goals resonate with our deepest aspirations, it is important to regularly evaluate and reassess them. As individuals and organizations evolve, so do our aspirations. By periodically reviewing our goals, we can make necessary adjustments to ensure they remain aligned with our vision. This ongoing process of reflection and refinement enables us to stay on track and continue progressing towards our deepest aspirations.

SMART Goals and Beyond

SMART, (specific, measurable, attainable, realistic and time bound) a concept introduced in 1981, remains the go-to model for goal setting, despite its intended use as a guide for managers in their writing objectives. SMART came under fire again in 2021 when Mark

Murphy, CEO of Leadership IQ, released the results of a SMART goal-setting study. The study surveyed 12,801 people and found that those who went above and beyond their SMART goals achieved greater results. "For the vast majority of our time," Murphy says, "SMART goal-setting serves as a hindrance to, rather than a facilitator of, courageous action." SMART goals encourage us to "play it safe" and "be within our wheelhouse" (be measurable and realistic).

The concept of SMART goals, which stands for Specific, Measurable, Achievable, Relevant, and Time-bound goals, is a widely recognized framework that helps individuals set clear and actionable objectives. By defining goals using these criteria, individuals can increase their chances of success and effectively track their progress. This framework can be adapted to suit ambitious pursuits by following a few key steps.

Firstly, when setting specific goals, it is important to clearly define what you want to achieve. This involves identifying the desired outcome, breaking it down into smaller milestones, and understanding the underlying purpose behind your pursuit. For example, if your ambitious pursuit is to start a successful business, a specific goal could be to establish a profitable online store within six months.

Secondly, measurable goals enable individuals to track their progress and determine whether they are on the right path. By establishing measurable criteria, such as revenue targets, customer acquisition numbers, or product development milestones, you can objectively assess your advancement. This allows you to make informed adjustments or celebrate milestones along the way.

Thirdly, achievable goals are realistic and feasible within the given resources and constraints. It is essential to evaluate the available time, skills, and resources needed to accomplish your pursuit. Setting goals that are too far-fetched or beyond your control may lead to frustration and discouragement. By ensuring your goals are attainable, you can maintain motivation and progress steadily.

Relevance is another crucial aspect of goal setting. Your goals should align with your overarching vision and values. Consider how your pursuit fits into your long-term aspirations and personal growth. By setting goals that are relevant to your ambitions, you can maintain focus and ensure that your efforts are in line with your desired outcome.

Lastly, time-bound goals provide a sense of urgency and create a clear deadline for achievement. By establishing specific timeframes for each goal, you can prioritize tasks, allocate resources effectively, and maintain momentum. This helps prevent procrastination and ensures consistent progress towards your ambitious pursuits.

The SMART goals framework offers a practical approach to goal setting that can be adapted to suit ambitious pursuits. By setting specific, measurable, achievable, relevant, and time-bound goals, individuals can increase their chances of success and effectively track their progress. Whether you are pursuing personal or professional ambitions, applying this framework can provide clarity, focus, and motivation on your journey towards achievement.

Crafting goals that are both inspiring and attainable requires careful consideration of the importance of specificity, measurement, and realistic challenges. By incorporating these elements into goal-setting, individuals and organizations can set themselves up for success and ensure that their aspirations are grounded in reality.

Specificity is crucial when crafting goals as it provides clarity and direction. Vague or ambiguous goals can lead to confusion and a lack of focus. On the other hand, specific goals outline exactly what needs to be achieved, leaving no room for interpretation. This allows individuals to better understand what is expected of them and enables them to take targeted actions towards achieving their goals.

Measurement is another key aspect of goal-setting. Without a way to measure progress, it becomes difficult to determine whether goals are being met or if adjustments need to be made. By establishing clear metrics or milestones, individuals can track their progress and make necessary adjustments along the way. Measurement also provides a sense of accountability and motivates individuals to stay on track towards their goals.

Realistic challenges are essential in crafting goals that are both inspiring and attainable. While it is important to dream big and set ambitious goals, it is equally important to ensure that these goals are within reach. Setting goals that are too lofty or unrealistic can lead to frustration and demotivation. By considering the resources, capabilities, and constraints at hand, individuals can set goals that are challenging yet realistic, increasing the likelihood of success.

Crafting inspiring and attainable goals requires a balance between ambition and pragmatism. By incorporating specificity, measurement, and realistic challenges into goal-setting, individuals and organizations can set themselves up for success. With clear direction, a means to measure progress, and goals that are within reach, individuals can be motivated and empowered to achieve their aspirations.

Breakdown into Actionable Steps

Breaking down big goals into smaller, actionable steps is an important process that can help individuals and organizations achieve success. By breaking down a big goal into smaller, more manageable tasks, it becomes easier to track progress, stay motivated, and make steady progress towards the overall objective.

To begin the process of breaking down big goals, it is helpful to start by clearly defining the main objective. This could be anything from starting a business, completing a project, or accomplishing a personal milestone. Once the main goal is established, it's important to take some time to think about the specific actions and tasks that need to be completed in order to achieve that goal.

One effective approach is to start by brainstorming a list of all the tasks that need to be done in order to reach the big goal. This could include things like conducting research, creating a plan, securing resources, and executing specific actions. It's important to be as specific and detailed as possible when creating this list, as it will serve as the foundation for breaking down the goal into smaller steps.

Once the list of tasks is complete, it's time to prioritize and organize them into smaller, actionable steps. One way to do this is by categorizing tasks based on their urgency, importance, or dependencies. For example, some tasks may need to be completed before others can be started, while others may have specific deadlines or time constraints.

After categorizing the tasks, it's helpful to assign due dates or deadlines to each step. This helps create a sense of urgency and keeps the momentum going. It's also important to consider any potential obstacles or challenges that may arise during the process and plan accordingly. This could include allocating additional time or resources to certain tasks, or seeking support and assistance from others.

As the smaller steps are defined and organized, it's important to track progress and make adjustments as needed. This could involve creating a project timeline or using a task management tool to keep track of completed tasks and upcoming deadlines. Regularly reviewing and updating the plan can help ensure that the goals remain achievable and realistic.

Prioritization and Focus

In the relentless pursuit of success, one of the paramount principles that sets achievers apart is the ability to prioritize goals and maintain unwavering focus. This cornerstone practice serves as a guiding light, steering individuals through the labyrinth of tasks, distractions, and competing interests, ensuring that efforts are channeled towards the most significant objectives.

The significance of prioritizing goals lies in its ability to provide a clear roadmap for personal and professional growth. In a world inundated with options and opportunities, the discerning individual understands the necessity of singling out those pursuits that align most closely with their overarching aspirations. This intentional selection not only conserves valuable time and resources but also sharpens the focus on endeavors that promise the greatest returns.

Prioritization serves as a strategic filter, sieving through the myriad of tasks vying for attention. By assigning levels of importance to different goals, individuals can effectively streamline their efforts, concentrating on what truly matters. This process is akin to distilling the essence of ambition, extracting the core elements that will propel one forward on the path to success.

However, prioritization alone is incomplete without the unwavering focus to see those chosen goals through to fruition. In a world characterized by constant connectivity and an influx of stimuli, maintaining concentration has become an elusive skill. Yet, it is precisely this ability to resist the allure of immediate gratification and stay fixated on long-term objectives that separates the achievers from the aspirants.

Unwavering focus is the glue that binds commitment to action. It is the force that propels individuals through challenges, setbacks, and the inevitable detours that life presents. Without this steadfast concentration, even the most well-prioritized goals can become mere fragments of unrealized potential.

The significance of maintaining unwavering focus becomes apparent when we consider the nature of achievement. Success is not a sprint but a marathon, demanding sustained effort and dedication. It requires weathering storms, navigating uncharted territories, and persisting when others falter. In such a journey, focus acts as a compass, always pointing towards the true north of one's aspirations.

Furthermore, unwavering focus cultivates a mindset of discipline and resilience. It instills the habit of finishing what is started, fostering a sense of accomplishment that propels individuals to tackle even more significant challenges. It is the secret sauce that transforms lofty goals from mere wishful thinking into tangible realities.

Conclusion

In this book, you have learned how to cultivate a wealthy mindset, set visionary goals, execute a master plan, infuse passion into your financial endeavors, and more.

The fortune formula presented here is an actionable step by step guide to unlocking the secret to financial success. It is a call to action that encourages you to embrace risk, adaptability, and adaptability. The principles outlined here go beyond initial success and dive into the essential aspects of how to sustain and grow wealth over time.

About The Author

Lucy Brooks is the New York Times and internationally author of <u>Youtube Creator's Bible</u>. <u>**Science, Christianity, and the AI Revolution: A Christian Perspective**</u>. <u>**Pips and Profits: Turning Market Moves into Wealth**</u>. A New York native, Lives in New Jersey with her husband, son, and dog.